Waffen-SS mountain troops in North Italy in late 1944. The men of this MG 42 team are wearing a fall/winter mottle camouflage smock of regulation pattern. The gunner wears the gebirgsmütze (mountain cap) while the others wear the camouflaged version of the einheitsmutze forage cap. Nearest man has rolled up zeltbahn (camouflage poncho).

𝕲𝖊𝖇𝖎𝖗𝖌𝖘𝖏𝖆̈𝖌𝖊𝖗

GERMAN MOUNTAIN TROOPS

Peter Chamberlain
and
Chris Ellis

ALMARK PUBLISHING CO. LTD., LONDON

First published—January 1973

ISBN 0 85524 109 8

Printed in Great Britain by
Vale Press Ltd., Mitcham, Surrey CR4 4HR,
for the publishers, Almark Publishing Co. Ltd.,
270 Burlington Road, New Malden,
Surrey KT3 4NL, England.

In the picturesque surroundings of the Bavarian Alps, this 7·5 cm Geb K15 is taken into action by its crew during 1939 manoeuvres. Crew are in 'drill book' positions, layer on left and detachment commander at right (with map case slung from belt). Next gun in battery is just visible on far right. (IWM-GER1216).

Introduction

UNLIKE other countries in Continental Europe, Germany had no specially trained mountain troops at the start of World War 1. France, Austria-Hungary, and Italy, by contrast, all had mountain units as part of their armies from the 1870s onward. Germany's late start was due to her military treaties with Austria-Hungary and Italy whose forces she relied on to secure mountain fronts in the event of a continental war. When war came in 1914, this policy soon proved embarassing, for Italy joined the Allied cause and became an enemy, while Austria-Hungary needed all available men to fight against the Russians in the east. Faced with this problem, Germany raised an *ad hoc* mountain force—the *Alpenkorps*—raised around a nucleus of volunteers who had peacetime ski or mountaineering experience, or who had lived or vacationed in mountain regions. Suitable guns for mountain use were scarce and a hasty assortment was mustered, mainly Krupp export products or light weapons drawn from German colonial units.

The *Alpenkorps*, despite its improvised nature, proved surprisingly

3

successful. On the Italian front, where the crack Alpini units of the Italian Army were expected to provide tough opposition, the Alpenkorps soon gained the upper hand. This was because the Italian generals held the Alpini units either in tactical reserve or guarding areas of particularly difficult terrain. The bulk of the mountain fronts were covered by ordinary troops with no specialised mountain warfare training. By contrast Alpenkorps companies were spread out to bolster up and lead the ordinary units which the Germans had, perforce, to employ all along the Alpine front. One such independent Alpenkorps company led the attack at Caporetto which resulted in the most important German victory of the war against Italy, the securing of the Isonzo Valley. The Alpenkorps company commander responsible for this feat, which involved storming and holding a dominating mountain ridge was a young lieutenant, Erwin Rommel, later to become the distinguished panzer general of World War 2.

The Treaty of Versailles in 1919 put major restrictions on the size of Germany's post-war army. Only one battalion of mountain infantry (now called *Gebirgsjäger*) was permitted, together with one mountain signal company, one mountain engineer company, and two mountain artillery batteries. These units themselves came under the control of a normal infantry division. In addition there were four light infantry battalions trained to fight in low mountains but these were not classed as true mountain troops.

Meanwhile Austria had kept up strong mountain forces after World War 1 and had no less than six full mountain infantry regiments and four independent mountain battalions, more than half her standing peacetime army. The new military command of the Third Reich realised from the accumulated experiences of World War 1 that mountain troops were important, and when Austria was annexed in 1938 the Austrian mountain units were all absorbed into the German Army. When war was declared in 1939 there was thus three full mountain divisions available for deployment (by contrast there were five still incomplete panzer divisions). By 1944 there were nine Army mountain divisions and four Waffen-SS mountain divisions. In addition there were under German command mountain divisions from Croatia, Hungary, Rumania, Bulgaria, and Italy, plus several independent mountain battalions and brigades. This made a grand total of 21 mountain divisions in all, or their equivalent in manpower. A number of light infantry (*Jäger*) divisions were trained for mountain operations as well. Besides all this there were some miscellaneous mountain units including Luftwaffe flakartillerie, Luftwaffe signal sections, and even police (*Polizei*) units trained for mountain operations.

Mountain divisions were deployed on all the main fighting fronts including Poland (Tatra Mountains and Carpathians), Norway, France (Vosges), the Balkans, Crete, Lapland, Russia (Caucasus), Italy (Apennines and Alps) and even Tunisia.

The laid down establishemnt for a mountain division (*Gebirgs-Division*) included a divisional HQ, a cycle battalion, two mountain infantry regiments, one mountain artillery regiment, one mountain engineer battalion, one anti-tank battalion, plus auxiliary units (medical, provost, supply, etc). There was some variation in actual establishment and manning scales, depending on the period and place. Some divisions were much under strength in the last year or so of the war. The tables opposite give theoretical strengths and equipment scales for a typical fully-equipped mountain division. Equipment of the 1943-44 period is quoted but there were variations for earlier or later periods.

The mountain infantry regiment (*Gebirgsjäger-Regiment*) formed the backbone of the mountain division and employed rather more men (with

4

Table 1: Composition and Strength

	Men	Motor-Cycles	Motor Vehicles	Horse-Drawn	Mules/Horses
Div HQ	200	12	26	—	20
Cycle Bn	551	57	37	—	—
Infantry Rgt (×2)	6,506	168	270	348	950
Arty Rgt	2,500	12	23	178	1,785
Engr Bn	1,049	42	96	64	256
A/T Bn	599	64	113	—	—
Signal Bn	476	28	102	7	56
Others	2,250	64	191	117	439
TOTALS	14,131	447	858	714	3,506

Table 2: Divisional Weapons

	Cycle Bn	2×Inf Rgts	Arty Regt	Engr Bn	A/A Bn	Sig Bn
Light MG	24	356	24	27	18	4
Hy MG	8	84	—	—	—	—
A/T rifles	—	72	—	—	—	—
20 mm AA/AT	—	—	—	—	12	—
37 mm Pak 37	3	24	—	—	—	—
50 mm Pak 38	—	—	—	—	24	—
50 mm Mrtr	6	54	—	—	—	—
81 mm Mrtr	3	36	—	—	—	—
75 mm How	2	12	36	—	—	—
105 mm How	—	—	12	—	—	—

Table 3: Composition of Infantry Regiment

	Men	Motor-Cycles	Motor Vehicles	Horse-Drawn	Mules/Horses
Regtl HQ	31	—	—	—	Varied with terrain
Signal Pln	43	—	—	—	
Mountain Bn (×3)	3,006	84	135	174	
A/T Coy	140	—	—	—	
Others	33	—	—	—	
TOTALS	3,253	84	135	174	Up to 475

Table 4: Infantry Regiment Weapons

	Mountain Inf Bn (×3)	A/T Coy	Total
SMG (MP 38, 40)	117	—	117
LMG (MG 34, 42)	172	6	178
HMG (MG 34, 42, or '08)	42	—	42
A/T Rifle (Pz B 38, 39)	36	—	36
37 mm Pak 37	—	12	12
50 mm Mortar	27	—	27
81 mm Mortar	18	—	18
75 mm Howitzer	6	—	6

lighter equipment and weapons) than an ordinary infantry regiment. The actual strength could and did vary but a typical infantry regiment at full establishment is shown in tables 3 and 4.

The authors wish to thank D. Nash, Fred Vos and the Imperial War Museum, London, for assistance in the selection of pictures.

The basic service dress for all Army and Waffen-SS mountain troops was the same as for the parent arm except that cloth anklet-type puttees and climbing boots replaced the usual leather knee-boot or ankle boot. The standard service black ankle boot was worn, however, instead of climbing boots in non-mountain terrain. The distinctive peaked forage cap (Gebirgs-mütze) was also unique to mountain troops until 1942, but a cap based on the mountain cap design was then adopted for universal military use. The peaked Gebirgsmütze cap was in turn derived from the Austrian mountain troops uniform which dated from well before World War 1. Before 1939 the German mountain troops sometimes wore cloth wrap-around puttees which reached almost to the knee, another clothing style which was still to be seen in the early part of the war and, again, derived from Austrian practice. These two men are demonstrating a method of carrying an injured man while on skis, using the ski sticks as a seat slung from the carrier's belt. The star arm badge denotes a senior private (Oberjäger). (IWM-MH12818).

ABOVE: Moutain troops had a distinctive badge featuring an Edelweiss mountain flower. In white metal it was carried on the left side of the Gebirgsmütze. On the service tunic it was worn on the right sleeve within an embroidered design. The men of this MG 42 light machine gun team are wearing the calico windjacket, a double breasted loose fitting coat in sage green which is rarely seen in pictures as it was issued only on a 10% strength basis. The gloves are dark field grey, in wool. RIGHT: Waffen-SS mountain troops wore the normal service dress with customary distinctions and rank badges. This Unterscharführer has the national emblem in its customary place on the left arm. Note collar patch rank insignia. This NCO is an instructor demonstrating the use of an ice axe and crampons at a mountain warfare school. These mountaineering items were, of course, widely used.

ABOVE: A MG 34 used on its tripod mount in the heavy machine gun role. The crew are wearing the Gebirgsmütze forage cap and normal field grey service dress. BELOW LEFT: Gebirgsjäger personnel wore a white metal representation of an Edelweiss (mountain flower) on the left side of the Gebirgsmütze cap. BELOW RIGHT: Jäger personnel wore a similar style of badge, from 1942, depicting oak leaves.

ABOVE: General de Gebirgstruppen Ringel (left) commanded 5th Gebirgsjäger Division at Crete in June 1941. Here he talks to men of his command who distinguished themselves in action. The general is wearing the mountain troops arm badge and the braid shoulder straps of his rank. The nearest soldier is a senior NCO (Oberfeldwebel) who is also a Bergführer (mountain guide), denoted by the enamel Edelweiss badge on his breast pocket. This was a key specialist qualification. The white outer ring carried the wording 'Heeresbergführer' (Army mountain leader). The other badges on the breast pockets visible are wound badges. BELOW LEFT: A close view of the mountain trooops embroidered arm badge. The flower was white with yellow centre and green stalk and leaves, while the outer circle in grey depicted twisted ropes. BELOW RIGHT: The Jäger troops embroidered arm badge, depicting oakleaves and acorn in light green with brown twig and green rope surround. The mountain troops badge was introduced in 1939 and the Jäger badge in 1942. Jäger formations were sometimes used in a mountain fighting role.

RIGHT: *Special mountain police units were raised to guard installations in mountainous regions, especially in occupied territories. These were from the Gendarmerie (in Germany) or State Police (Polizei) in occupied lands. Though not part of the armed forces, mountain police units often acted in close liaison with mountain troops and wore the Gebirgsmütze (sometimes with the Edelweiss badge on the cap) and cloth puttees, though the man shown here is not actually wearing the latter. The rest of the uniform was standard field grey police service dress. The arm badge featured a national eagle and laurel wreath design.*
BELOW, LEFT: *The Army Gebirgsjäger shown here wears service dress with the early style of wrap-around cloth puttees, generally discarded by 1939-40. BELOW, CENTRE: SS-VT (later Waffen-SS) Gebirgsjäger of 1939 wearing the pre-war earth grey SS-VT service dress which featured an open collar tunic. This dress was being replaced by a field grey version with closed collar by 1939. BELOW, RIGHT: Luftwaffe personnel manned some mountain Flakartillerie and signal units and wore the normal blue-grey Luftwaffe service dress with a Gebirgsmütze cap and puttees (US Official).*

ABOVE, LEFT: The calico windjacket was of proofed material, sage green in colour and loose fitting for wear over basic equipment if desired. It was issued only to about 10% of personnel and thus is not widely seen in photographs of mountain troops. Rank badges were carried on normal pattern detachable shoulder straps. ABOVE, CENTRE: The winter sheepskin coat, fur hat, and fur boots were issued for special duties only, particularly to sentries and other watchkeepers like radio operators in exposed posts. ABOVE, RIGHT: The two piece reversible winter suit was issued (to all arms not just mountain troops) in the winter of 1942-43 on the Russian front. Of heavy multi-layer windproof/waterproof material, it was white one side and field-grey or 'splinter' camouflage the other. Coloured arm bands were for indentity purposes (US Official). BELOW: Early form of snow camouflage was a loose hooded coverall with sleeves, worn over normal service dress. Skiers are pictured in 1940.

Unique item of clothing for mountain troops was the reversible anorak first issued in 1939. It was white on one side and sage green (later camouflaged) on the other. It had a drawstring waist, drawstring hood, elasticated cuffs and two breast pockets, with the usual national eagle emblem in the early days; later this was omitted. Picture above shows two men wearing the anorak white side out above the snowline. Picture below (IWM-GER 1206) shows MG 34 gunner with hood up and drawstring tied.

ABOVE: The same anorak shown opposite is here being worn in both camouflaged form (second and third men) and plain sage green form (first man). In the case of the first man the white inner colour is just visible. These are men of an infantry ski company in Abruzzi province, Italy, late 1943. They travel light with their packs carried by the accompanying mules and horses.

LEFT: In the winter of 1943-44, a new windproof anorak suit was issued (though old anoraks remained in use). This suit consisted of both a coat and trousers, all made of rayon triple layer material which was both windproof and water repellent. The suit was reversible, white one side (far left) and tan-brown on the other (left). There were three breast pockets, a drawstring waist and button-up hood (US Official).

This 1940 picture shows part of a Gebirgsjäger infantry company on the march. Following mountain trails, the infantry invariably moved in file either by platoons or companies depending on the situation. The leading five men are a medium machine gun crew carrying the barrel, carriage, ammunition and ancillary equipment for the MG 08 machine gun (at this time the MG 34 was still not on universal issue). Note the Bergen style rucksacks and also the ammunition box on the back of the second man. The MG team, and the following rifle squad each have an issue of ice axes. Apart from being put to conventional mountaineering use, the ice axes were also used to make MG positions, etc. The unit shown is marching at very close spacing. In combat areas the intervals between individual men would be much greater—as much as 100 metres— depending on the terrain and tactical situation. For instance in the presence of enemy air activity the spacing between men would be at its maximum.

ABOVE: Ice axes are here seen stuck in the snow on the left, having been used to level off a site for a MG 34 of a medium machine gun company. This picture dates from the Norwegian campaign of April 1940. This gun is set up in a typical defence position on a ridge commanding a mountain pass. Part of defence line, only a lookout mans the weapon.

LEFT: Though there was no armour element on the establishment of mountain divisions, armoured units were attached when tactical requirements demanded. In low mountain country roads and tracks were poor and often blocked. In this view, men of a mountain division engineer company are clearing a road to allow the passage of two 7·5 cm Stu G 40 assault guns which are supporting forward infantry units in the Caucasus near Tuapse, Russia 1944.

RIGHT: All German mountain troops received training in rock climbing and had to meet a laid down level of proficiency. Much of the climbing work encountered was of the 'scrambling' variety (as shown here) where nimble use of hands and feet was sufficient. However, conventional rope climbing technique was also employed where necessary—and it was encouraged when units could achieve an element of surprise by scaling what might appear to the enemy to be an 'impassable' ridge or rock face. For the difficult faces a Bergführer or other experienced NCO used normal 'tension climbing' (with pitons and links) to scale a face and set up a rope climb for the following men. For sheer faces the Bilgeri climb was favoured—this used two ropes in stirrup fashion hauling up one man at a time.

LEFT: Dogs were used by mountain troops mainly as light supply carriers. They carried in particular medical packs, but machine gun teams also used them to carry belts of ammunition. This dog is employed in the latter rôle, having a canvas 'bread bag' strapped each side of his shoulders. Dogs were sometimes used to seek out tracks up the mountain. A few messenger dogs were also used. Pictures on this page show troops scaling the heights of Montenegro, Jugoslavia, in January 1944 during operations against General Tito's partisan forces.

LEFT: Semaphore signalling was frequently used in steep terrain, particularly by leading infantry units as bulky radio equipment could not be transported easily up difficult climbs. These men are signalling across a pass in the Caucasian mountains.

RIGHT: The earliest type of radio set carried by mountain troops was the Tornister Funkgërat d2 which took a three-man crew and (at 78 lbs) was carried in two loads. Leading man carries the transmitter/receiver unit (with tall aerial just visible behind left shoulder) while the second man, linked by cable, carries the battery power box. This set had a two mile voice range and 10 mile morse range. By 1943 a simpler 29 lb one-man pack (Feldfunk Sprecher b and c) had been issued.

ABOVE: Mountain divisions used standard Army signal equipment for main communications, adapted for carriage on pack saddles by mules or horses. This signal unit carries a ten-line command switchboard in panniers on the nearest mule with the cable reels on the mule next ahead. On top of the saddle is a reel on a packboard which was attached to a signaller's back (RIGHT) for paying out either on foot or on skis as appropriate. BELOW: Close view of a pack horse carrying cable reels in a simple wood frame pack saddle. Note officer on right with map case and wearing jackboots.

LEFT: Another item of signal equipment was this pedal operated Telefunken generator which provided power for the standard types of radio set. Here one man pedals while the operator transmits a signal by Morse. This pedal generator had been used pre-war by the forestry service and its portability lent itself to mountain use.

BELOW: Casualty evacuation at its most extreme involved advanced cliff scaling techniques. The special carrier shown here was made of proofed canvas and was issued to all units for roping casualties down sheer faces.

BELOW: A rescue dog of a mountain medical team. The St Bernard was favoured. Haversacks and standard canteens were carried in a haversack. Dogs sought out injured men ahead of the medical personnel.

ABOVE: Besides the normal hazards of war, mountain troops were subjected to the natural risks inherent in all climbing and mountaineering activities. The German mountain medical units were well equipped to deal with frostbite, rope burns, snow blindness, falls, fractures, and altitude sickness as well as wounds. This mule carries the medical officer's supply box together with a rolled 'ward tent' (16½ × 3 ft high sides, ridged) and an 'operating tent' (16½ × 5 ft high sides, ridged). Both tents were of lightweight camouflage material, each rolled in two halves.

LEFT: For casualty evacuation in winter the ski stretcher was employed and came in component parts carried either by men or mules. It could be towed by skiers or a mule, or hauled by a four-man team.

RIGHT: Unicycle stretcher was a special item of mountain troops equipment. It had folding legs to hold it upright as an operating table. Weight was 25 lb and it broke into component parts.

Mountain artillery units have a requirement for light but effective pieces which can fulfill all the rôles of normal artillery but can also be broken into easily portable loads for handling in difficult terrain. The German 7·5 cm Geb K15 was the main howitzer in use and is generally considered to have been the best mountain gun in service anywhere during World War 2. Here the carriage of one of these guns is hauled up a sheer face to its firing position, using block, tackle, and the standard service rig of a tree trunk boom suitably positioned.

ABOVE: The 7·5 cm Geb K15 (a Czech Skoda design) broke down into six horse or mule loads (or seven when the shield was used). In this view a pack horse carries the gun carriage while the second horse visible carries the wheels. Note the spades strapped on the side of the horse's harness. The horse/mule driver was required by regulations to carry his rifle slung over his chest when handling his animal.

ABOVE: A good close view of the standard German pack saddle and harness. The two yokes carry and distribute the load, taking the necessary attachment to facilitate holding the particular load. In the case of the 7·5 cm gun barrel shown only straps on top of the yokes are necessary. When used to carry stores, a wicker basket was fitted to the side legs of the yokes (one basket each side of the animal) strapped where the gun's ramrod is strapped in this picture.

ABOVE: 1940 picture shows a 7·5 cm Geb K15 team on the march. Lead mule carries trail and wheels, second the barrel. Third and fourth carry the two-part shield plus ammunition boxes and wicker mats. BELOW: Close view of shield on assembled weapon. In later war period this was omitted to lighten the total load.

RIGHT: An excellent view of a 7·5 cm Geb K15 in action pictured at the moment of firing and on full recoil. Note the gunner on right pulling lanyard. Small size of weapon is apparent by contrast to the men. Shield is omitted on this example. Mobility was essential above snow line for gun position was quickly revealed by cloud of snow put up when firing. Crew are wearing the calico windjacket and gunlayer (at left) has his cap reversed to keep peak clear of telescope when sighting.

LEFT: The Germans purchased 7·5 cm Geb K15 guns from Skoda prewar (as did other nations) and supplemented their stocks by capture from Czechoslovakia and other occupied countries. A typical captured type used in some numbers was the French Schneider 7·5 cm M1919, very similar to the Skoda weapon and complete with folding trail to facilitate handling on narrow mountain tracks.

ABOVE: The 7·5 cm Geb G36 was a German designed weapon with a split trail which gave it a 70° elevation and enabled it to be used as a howitzer. Ostensibly it was a replacement for the 7·5 cm Geb K15 but did not, in fact, oust the earlier weapon which was lighter and hence more mobile. The 7·5 cm Geb G36 weighed 1,600 pounds and had a 10,000 yard range. This picture shows it emplaced at 18,400 feet in murky weather on Mount Elbras, Caucasus. Just visible are wicker mats beneath wheels to give a grip on snow, ice, and mud. BELOW: The compact size of the 7·5 cm Geb K15 is emphasised in this view which shows the crew quickly assembling the weapon for action. It weighed 1,386 pounds and ranged up to 7,315 yards.

ABOVE: Another view of the 7·5 cm Geb G36, this time being manhandled into position for firing. The disc wheels could be replaced by a skid chassis for handling in deep snow. This weapon broke into six loads for mule transport. BELOW: The 7·5 cm le Geb IG 18 was a howitzer version of the K15 with split trail and revised cradle for high angle fire. This one is on the Russian Front, 1944.

ABOVE: The heavy howitzer used by the German mountain artillery was a captured ex-Czech type, the Skoda M16/19. In German hands it was designated 10·5 cm Geb H (t). Several other countries in the 1939-40 period used this weapon including France, Poland, and Austria. It was too heavy for mule transport and broke into three cart loads, for towing by horse or manpower. Two loads are shown on their carriage, the third being the barrel and cradle on its own. BELOW: The 10·5 cm Geb H40 was purpose-designed as a lightweight howitzer for use by both mountain and airborne troops. It was towed in three loads on carts and broke into 12 parts for man-handling.

ABOVE: The 10·5 cm Geb H40 at full recoil at the moment of firing, with the crew reacting to its vicious roar. Note rounds laid out ready for use. Barrel life was over 15,000 rounds. LEFT: The weapon at full elevation reached 70°, as shown here. Wheels were attached directly to the trail giving an ungainly 'pigeon toe' appearance when the piece was emplaced.

A ski patrol of mountain infantrymen have left their skis on the mountain track (just to the right, off picture) while they peer cautiously over the edge of a ridge on the lookout for the enemy. They are wearing greatcoats and carry Bergen type rucksacks. Some 25% of the men of a mountain division were expected to be skiers. A six week course for trainee skiers was held at the various mountain warfare schools. In practice many divisions had more than 25% skiers since many conscripts who joined the Army elected to join mountain divisions if they already had pre-war skiing experience.

Principal Mountain Guns

Designation	Weight in pounds (firing)	Max. Range (yards)	Weight of shell (HE)	Pack loads
*7·5 cm Gem K238(f)	1,496	10,450	14	7-8 mules
7·5 cm Geb K15	1,386	7,315	12	6 mules (or 7 with shield)
7·5 cm Geb G36	1,600	10,116	13	6 mules
10 cm Geb H16	2,717	9,020	35	3 cart loads
10·5 cm Geb H40	3,360	13,807	?	3 carts (or 12 smaller loads)
*10·5 cm Geb H 322(f)	1,650	8,690	27	8 mules
2 cm Geb Flak 38	1,013			27 man loads

(*captured French types, Schneider models)

In addition to the special mountain guns listed above there were a number of other light weapons used by mountain divisions. Among these were the following: 5 cm Pak 38, 3·7 cm Pak 37, 42/28 mm 4·7 cm le Pak 41, 28/20 mm s. Pz B 41 (all used variously by mountain anti-tank battalions and companies); 5 cm le Mrs, 8·1 cm Mrs (mortar platoons and companies); 15 cm Nebelwerfer 41 (late war period, rocket launcher used by mountain artillery regiments); the 7·5 cm le Geb IG 18 was a light howitzer version of the 7·5 cm Geb K15 used by infantry gun companies—details generally as for the K15.

The 2 cm Geb Flak 38 was a special lightweight version of the 2 cm Flak 38 specially for use by AA units in mountain divisions. It had a secondary rôle as a light anti-tank gun. Extensive use of metal pressings kept the weight of this gun as low as possible. It could be towed by mule or horse, or broken into 27 man loads, maximum weight 90 pounds. Wheels were removed for emplacement and gun sat on cruciform legs.

Mountain divisions had a proportion of motor trucks, plus lightweight vehicles like the VW Kubelwagen, the NSU Kettenrad tractor and motor cycles, but all these were mostly restricted to lowland use. The main form of transport was provided by horse-drawn wagons and mules or pack horses. The standard general service wagon carried stores and the infantry battalions had the MG Doppelwagen 36, a steel, rubber-tyred, articulated cart as shown above. This one carries the MG 34s of a support platoon rigged to give AA fire if required on the march.

LEFT: The cycle battalion of a mountain division fulfilled the reconnaissance rôle with a mixture of pedal cycles and motor cycles. Here is the standard cycle fitted to carry the 5 cm light mortar. The MG 34 could be similarly carried.

RIGHT: Mountain troops were trained to supplement their own limited transport by local acquisition—either of civil vehicles and carts or enemy equipment. Here a Universal Carrier, recently captured, is used by mountain troops in Crete in 1941.

Rivers, gorges, and other natural obstacles abound in mountain areas. The engineer battalion carried minimal equipment, and the standard bridge and pontoon gear was not included on strength but was supplied from Corps or Army resources when needed, as here, to bridge wide deep rivers. The divisional engineers were fully trained in its use.

Divisional engineers did not normally carry standard service bridging equipment since it was too bulky for pack or horse-drawn transportation in steep mountainous regions. Motor-powered saws and other quality tools were provided to facilitate maximum utilisation of local resources, mainly trees and timber. *ABOVE:* This spar trestle bridge, decked with planks (which the engineers did carry) was the normal type used to get mules and men across a wide mountain torrent. The spars are from trees which grew near the crossing point.

RIGHT: Rope and plank bridge across a gorge or wide stream was favoured when only men were required to cross; it was quick to rig.

Publisher's Note

This book covers mainly the weapons, equipment, uniform and activities peculiar to mountain troops. Small arms and infantry support weapons used by the mountain divisions were the same as for normal infantry units and these are illustrated and described in more detail in a companion 'Wehrmacht Illustrated' book *Panzer-Grenadiers*.